TRADE CAREERS
MASON

by Joanne Mattern

pogo

Ideas for Parents and Teachers

Pogo Books let children practice reading informational text while introducing them to nonfiction features such as headings, labels, sidebars, maps, and diagrams, as well as a table of contents, glossary, and index.

Carefully leveled text with a strong photo match offers early fluent readers the support they need to succeed.

Before Reading

- "Walk" through the book and point out the various nonfiction features. Ask the student what purpose each feature serves.
- Look at the glossary together. Read and discuss the words.

Read the Book

- Have the child read the book independently.
- Invite him or her to list questions that arise from reading.

After Reading

- Discuss the child's questions. Talk about how he or she might find answers to those questions.
- Prompt the child to think more. Ask: Would you like to be a mason? What do you like about this trade career?

Pogo Books are published by Jump!
5357 Penn Avenue South
Minneapolis, MN 55419
www.jumplibrary.com

Copyright © 2025 Jump! International copyright reserved in all countries. No part of this book may be reproduced in any form without written permission from the publisher.

Library of Congress Cataloging-in-Publication Data

Names: Mattern, Joanne, 1963- author.
Title: Mason / by Joanne Mattern.
Description: Minneapolis, MN: Jump!, Inc., [2025]
Series: Trade careers | Includes index.
Audience: Ages 7-10
Identifiers: LCCN 2023058787 (print)
LCCN 2023058788 (ebook)
ISBN 9798892131612 (hardcover)
ISBN 9798892131629 (paperback)
ISBN 9798892131636 (ebook)
Subjects: LCSH: Masonry—Vocational guidance—Juvenile literature.
Classification: LCC TH5325 .M38 2025 (print)
LCC TH5325 (ebook)
DDC 693/.1023—dc23/eng/20240130
LC record available at https://lccn.loc.gov/2023058787
LC ebook record available at https://lccn.loc.gov/2023058788

Editor: Alyssa Sorenson
Designer: Anna Peterson
Content Consultant: Rebecca Nohava, Brickmason

Photo Credits: Gus And/Shutterstock, cover (wall); addkm/Shutterstock, cover (trowel); Bet_Noire/iStock, 1; J.NATAYO/Shutterstock, 3; Phovoir/Shutterstock, 4; Hanna Taniukevich/Shutterstock, 5; JaneHYork/Shutterstock, 6-7; TORSupachai/Shutterstock, 7 (trowel); nik7ch/Shutterstock, 7 (chisel); Dede80/Shutterstock, 7 (walling hammer); AnotherPerfectDay/Shutterstock, 7 (tape measure); Tomahawk Power, LLC, 7 (screed); goodze/iStock, 7 (masonry saw); OlegSam/Shutterstock, 7 (level); gutaper/Getty, 8-9; lunamarina/Shutterstock, 10-11; wimammoth/Shutterstock, 12 (bricks); Michael Burrell/iStock, 12 (cap); Yuri_Arcurs/Getty, 13; Dmitry Kalinovsky/Shutterstock, 14-15, 18; Diego Cervo/Shutterstock, 16-17; Tasha-photo/Shutterstock, 19; photosvit/iStock, 20-21; Shawn Hempel/Shutterstock, 23.

Printed in the United States of America at Corporate Graphics in North Mankato, Minnesota.

TABLE OF CONTENTS

CHAPTER 1
What Is a Mason?......................................4

CHAPTER 2
Learning the Trade....................................12

CHAPTER 3
Where They Work....................................18

ACTIVITIES & TOOLS
Try This!..22
Glossary..23
Index...24
To Learn More...24

CHAPTER 1

WHAT IS A MASON?

Masons build and fix things made of **concrete**, brick, and stone. They might make a stone walkway. They might fix broken bricks on a chimney. Look around. Masonry work is everywhere!

Masons build brick walls. How? First, they set up **forms**. They pour concrete into them. This will be the wall's **base**. Masons **level** the concrete. They wait for it to dry.

The base is hard. A mason starts laying bricks. He uses a **trowel**. He spreads **mortar** on the base. Then he puts the first row of bricks on top. He makes sure the bricks are in a straight line. Next, he spreads another layer of mortar. He lays more bricks.

TAKE A LOOK!

Masons use many tools. What are some? Take a look!

trowel: spreads mortar

chisel: chips away and shapes pieces of stone, brick, or concrete

walling hammer: chips away pieces of stone

tape measure: measures how long something is

screed: smooths and levels wet concrete

masonry saw: cuts concrete, brick, and stone

level: makes sure a surface is exactly horizontal or vertical

CHAPTER 1 | 7

Some mortar squeezes out. The mason uses a trowel. He wipes the extra mortar away. It is time for the next row of bricks. He does this until the wall is done!

DID YOU KNOW?

Masons work with rough materials. Gloves protect their hands. Masons cut brick, stone, and concrete. Small pieces fly up. Safety glasses protect their eyes. Hard hats protect their heads.

CHAPTER 1 9

This mason builds a stone wall.
How? He uses a walling hammer.
It chips away parts of the stones.
This is how he shapes them.
The stones fit like puzzle pieces.
Mortar sticks them together.

DID YOU KNOW?

There are different kinds of masons. Cement masons work with concrete. Brickmasons work with brick. Stonemasons build with stone.

CHAPTER 2
LEARNING THE TRADE

Do you want to be a mason? First, you must pass high school.

apprentice

Then you will need to work as an **apprentice**. This can last three or four years. An experienced mason will teach you the **trade**. You can also take classes.

CHAPTER 2

Masons lift heavy objects. They stand, bend, and kneel all day. They need to be in good shape.

Masons pay attention to details. Why? They need to put bricks, stones, and concrete blocks in just the right place. They make sure the finished project looks good.

How much material do masons need for a project? They find out. How? They read **blueprints**. They measure. They use math skills.

blueprints

CHAPTER 2 17

CHAPTER 3
WHERE THEY WORK

Masons often work outside. They help build homes and places around town.

Masons watch the weather. If it will rain, they cover their project. Why? Mortar should not get wet. Extreme heat or cold can also affect it. It may not dry or set right.

CHAPTER 3

Masons are busy builders. Some build roads. Others build dams. There are many masonry jobs. Would you like to be a mason?

DID YOU KNOW?

Some masons work on tall buildings. They wear **harnesses**. Why? These catch them if they fall.

CHAPTER 3

ACTIVITIES & TOOLS

TRY THIS!

BUILD A WALL

Make a wall like a mason!

What You Need:
- flat wooden blocks
- modeling clay
- small plastic shovel
- plastic knife

❶ Use the small plastic shovel to spread modeling clay across the top of one block.

❷ Put another block on top. Press it into the clay.

❸ Use the knife to scrape off extra clay that squeezed out.

❹ Put clay on the end of one block.

❺ Place another block on the end. Press it into the clay. Scrape off any extra clay.

❻ Repeat these steps until you have made a wall!

GLOSSARY

apprentice: Someone who learns a skill by working with an expert.

base: The lowest or supporting part of something.

blueprints: Detailed design plans that show how something should be built.

concrete: A building material made from a mixture of sand, gravel, cement, and water, which becomes very hard when it dries.

forms: Molds in which wet concrete is poured.

harnesses: Straps used to connect people to something and keep them safe.

level: To make something flat and even.

mortar: A mixture of lime, sand, water, and cement that is used to hold bricks and stones together.

trade: A job that requires working with the hands or with machines.

trowel: A hand tool with a flat blade.

INDEX

apprentice 13
base 5, 6
blueprints 16
brick 4, 5, 6, 7, 9, 10, 15
chimney 4
concrete 4, 5, 7, 9, 10, 15
dams 20
forms 5
gloves 9
hard hats 9
harnesses 20
materials 9, 16
math 16
measures 7, 16
mortar 6, 7, 9, 10, 19
roads 20
safety glasses 9
stone 4, 7, 9, 10, 15
tools 7
trowel 6, 7, 9
walkway 4
weather 19

TO LEARN MORE

Finding more information is as easy as 1, 2, 3.
❶ Go to www.factsurfer.com
❷ Enter "mason" into the search box.
❸ Choose your book to see a list of websites.